It's Laugh o'Clock

Would you Rather?

Christmas Edition

Funny Scenarios, Wacky Choices
and Hilarious Situations
For Kids and Family

With Fun Illustrations

Riddleland

TABLE OF CONTENTS

Riddleland Bonus

Join our **Facebook Group** at **Riddleland for Kids**
to get daily jokes and riddles.

https://pixelfy.me/riddlelandbonus

Thank you for buying this book. As a token of our appreciation,
we would like to offer a special bonus—a collection of
50 original jokes, riddles, and funny stories.

INTRODUCTION

"May you never be too grown up to search the skies on Christmas Eve."

~ Unknown

Are you ready to make some decisions? **It's Laugh O'Clock - Would You Rather? Christmas Edition** is a collection of funny scenarios, wacky choices, and hilarious situations which offer alternative endings for kids and adults to choose among.

These questions are an excellent way to get a fun and exciting conversation started. Also, by asking "Why?" after a "Would you Rather . . . " question, learn a lot about the person, including their values and their thinking process.

We wrote this book because we want children to be encouraged to read more, think, and grow. As parents, we know that when children play games, they are being educated while having so much fun that they don't even realize they're learning and developing valuable life skills. "Would you Rather . . . " is one of our favorite games to play as a family. Some of the 'would you rather ...' scenarios have had us in fits of giggles, others have generated reactions such as: "Eeeeeuuuugh, that's gross!" and yet others really make us think, reflect and consider our own decisions.

Besides having fun, playing these questions have other benefits such as:

Enhancing Communication – This game helps children to interact, read aloud, and listen to others. It's a fun way for parents to get their children interacting with them without a formal, awkward conversation. The game can also help to get to know someone better and learn about their likes, dislikes, and values.

Building Confidence – The game encourages children to get used to pronouncing vocabulary, asking questions, and overcoming shyness.

Developing Critical Thinking – It helps children to defend and justify the rationale for their choices and can generate discussions and debates. Parents playing this game with young children can give them prompting questions about their answers to help them reach logical and sensible decisions.

Improving Vocabulary – Children will be introduced to new words in the questions, and the context of them will help them remember the words because the game is fun.

Encouraging Equality and Diversity – Considering other people's answers, even if they differ from your own, is important for respect, equality, diversity, tolerance, acceptance, and inclusivity. Some questions may get children to think outside the box and move beyond stereotypes associated with gender.

Would You Rather?
Christmas Edition

How do you play?

At least two players are needed to play this game. Face your opponent and decide who is **Santa Elf 1** and **Santa Elf 2**. If you have 3 or 4 players, you can decide which players belong to **Santa Helper 1** and **Santa Helper 2**. The goal of the game is to score points by making the other players laugh. The first player to a score of 10 points is the **Champion**.

What are the rules?

Santa Elf 1 starts first. Read the questions aloud and choose an answer. The same player will then explain why they chose the answer in the silliest and wackiest way possible. If the reason makes the **Santa Elf 2** laugh, then **Santa Elf 1** scores a funny point. Take turns going back and forth and write down the score.

How do you get started?

Flip a coin. The Player that guesses it correctly starts first.

Bonus Tip:

Making funny voices, silly dance moves or wacky facial expressions will make your opponent laugh!

Most Importantly:

Remember to have fun and enjoy the game!

Would you Rather...

Be a snowman with a carrot nose that
a reindeer keeps trying to eat

have a pet reindeer in your backyard that
you have to pooper scoop every day?

Have to make all new handmade ornaments for your
Christmas tree every year

cut strings of paper snowflake garland to cover your
whole house?

Would You Rather...

Be followed to school by
a super creepy group of really tiny snowmen

find a very quiet and very large snowman hiding
in your closet after school?

Have a giant blow up snowman in your front yard
who follows you with his eyes

a giant blowup Rudolph outside your window whose red
nose blinks through your bedroom window all night long?

Would You Rather...

Try to play in the snow with hands so hot that they melt the snow on contact

have hands so cold that you need to wear mittens year-round?

Have an enormous hot pink Christmas tree in the middle of your living room

wear a hot pink Santa suit to school for one day?

Would You Rather...

Have a lovable pet snowman who needs
to be rebuilt every day

OR

a pet abominable snowman who
chews on your pillow?

Open presents sitting next to a Christmas tree that plays
music and has lights that blink in rhythm

OR

have all the lights on your Christmas tree burn out
right before you open presents?

Would You Rather...

Get hit in the face with a snowball every time you don't know the answer to a question on your homework

OR

get hit in the face with a snowball every time you tell a lie?

Go to bed on a soft pillow that smells like a pine tree is in your nose

OR

sleep on a bundle of real poky pine tree branches?

Would You Rather...

Be turned into a snowman and cursed to spend the rest of winter outside until you melt into a puddle

have long icicles at the ends of your fingers instead of fingernails?

Get a ride to school in the back of Santa's supersonic sleigh

ride to school on the back of a flying reindeer who smells like the back of an old barn?

Would You Rather...

Be adopted by a family of snowmen and live
in a freezing cold house made of ice

have a pet coconut named "Coco" who goes with you
everywhere and has her very own little winter coat?

Have your teacher wear a Santa Claus suit
to school every day in December

grow a white fluffy beard like Santa Claus that you have
to shave every day in December?

Would You Rather...

Build a snowman using
dirty brown snow

using bunny poops for the eyes
on your snowman's face?

Take a family photo wearing the ugliest
Christmas sweater ever

take a really fancy family photo where a big piece of hair
is sticking out of your head in a wonky way but everyone
else looks fabulous?

Would You Rather...

Be able to shake beautifully patterned snowflakes
from your hair

spit perfectly round little snowballs out of your mouth?

Get pulled to school on a sled by your dad

go ice skating holding hands with your mom?

Would You Rather...

Wear a hat that is two sizes too big and
is always falling over your eyes

wear a pair of mismatched gloves, one that is too small and
squishes your hand and one that is too big and keeps falling off?

Do the polar plunge where
you dive into a cold lake or river in your swimsuit

get a big bear hug from someone who just did the polar
plunge into a cold lake or river?

Would You Rather...

Wear gloves that stick to everything
you touch outside

wear mittens that make your arms feel heavy because
they're super soggy and wet?

Spend your day chopping wood with an axe
for an old-fashioned fireplace

weaving an evergreen wreath for your front door?

Would You Rather...

Go outside with wet hair that freezes stiff in the cold and breaks off when the wind blows

shave your head bald and never wear a hat in the winter?

Eat a bowlful of marshmallows that have hard and crunchy pieces of candy cane in them

eat a handful of candy canes that are squishy like fresh marshmallows?

Would You Rather...

Wear a knitted scarf that smells like cinnamon wrapped tightly around your face

wear a soggy scarf wrapped tightly around your face?

Ride to school on a chilly school bus that doesn't have a working heater

walk to school on a really icy slippery sidewalk?

Would You Rather...

Try to make 100 paper snowflakes with
a pair of old rusty scissors

try to make 100 snowflakes using old cereal boxes
instead of paper?

Get chased around the playground all day by a
gingerbread cookie come to life

bake the most amazing looking gingerbread cookie that
smells like rotten milk?

Would You Rather...

Spend a whole day catching snowflakes and looking at them under a microscope

OR

stay outside all day during a blizzard trying to measure the snowfall with a ruler?

Spend Christmas Eve with your family singing Christmas carols outside around your whole neighborhood

OR

at the shopping mall wrapping presents for other people?

Would You Rather...

Only be able to eat snow for one whole day

only be able to suck on icicles for one whole day?

Have to give away one of your belongings
for every present you receive on Christmas

get to buy a new item of your choice for someone else for
every present you receive on Christmas?

Would You Rather...

Have a grumpy little pet gingerbread cookie named Ginger you absolutely can't eat

a rather large red and white striped candy cane growing out of your nose?

Try to make a creamy smoothie using hot chocolate and ice cubes

make a yummy banana and yellow snow smoothie?

Would You Rather...

Use a really tipsy ladder to put the head on top of your very tall snowman

have a giant chunk of ice fall off your roof and hit you hard in the head?

Build a snowman on a cold day using only your hands

shovel your driveway clean using only a dinner spoon?

Would You Rather...

Be able to freeze things by touching them
with your fingers

leave gooshy slushy footprints wherever you walk?

Go sledding while wearing nothing
on your bare feet

have a snowball fight while wearing
a pair of stinky socks on your hands?

Would You Rather...

Walk around with two giant blocks of ice
instead of feet

try to get through a school day with hands so frozen that
you can't move your fingers?

Spend the day digging tunnels through giant snow hills
like an ant in an ant farm

get lost in the tunnels you've dug and have to spend the
night inside them?

Would You Rather...

Play outside at recess in a blizzard where you can't see anything

have to stay inside at your desk with your head down instead?

Hibernate (sleep) all winter long like a grizzly bear

walk to school through deep snow drifts every day all winter long?

Would You Rather...

Wear a pair of gloves on the wrong hands

wear your boots on the wrong feet for a whole week?

Get so cold outside that your skin turns bright red
and stays that way all day

get so cold outside that your lips turn deep blue
and stay that way all day?

Would you Rather...

Be a papa penguin spending all of your time with an egg between your feet waiting for it to hatch

have snowshoes super glued to your feet so you can never take them off?

Have a giant stack of Christmas presents under a really sad and spindly Christmas tree

only get one Christmas present under a beautiful big evergreen Christmas tree?

Would you Rather...

Grow pine tree scented hair out of your ears

grow spiky pine needles instead of hair?

Open your Christmas presents with
one hand tied behind your back

open your Christmas presents using
only your feet?

Would You Rather...

Live in a really hot country where
it never ever snows

a country with so much snow that your school
is actually made out of snow?

Be transformed into Santa Claus with a large belly and white
beard, and his red and white outfit until Christmas Day?

be transformed into one of Santa's Elves working at his
toy factory until Christmas Eve?

Would You Rather...

Wear a pair of white socks that are now a dirty brown on your hands as mittens

a pair of wet and smelly mittens on your feet instead of socks?

Celebrate Christmas in a place with lots of sun and palm trees

in a place with beautiful winter snowflakes and shovels?

Would You Rather...

Wear a winter hat that makes your
head super itchy

a pair of snow pants that are too tight around the waist
so you have to suck in your stomach?

Eat a fruitcake sandwich - two pieces of fruitcake
with a sugar cookie in between

drink a peppermint, hot chocolate, and eggnog milkshake?

Would You Rather...

Skate at a turtle's crawling speed using
super dull ice skates

ski frighteningly fast down a hill on butter-coated skis?

Be the forgotten tenth reindeer who
is left out of all the Christmas stories

be the dog who has to pull the Grinch's sleigh
in Dr. Seuss's "How the Grinch Stole Christmas!"?

Would you Rather...

Have a snowball fight using
scoops of ice cream

a water gun fight using hot chocolate?

Eat a stack of pancakes drizzled
with eggnog

eat a candy cane dipped in maple syrup?

Would You Rather...

Burn your tongue on
a smoking hot cup of hot chocolate

take an ice-cold shower because your brother or sister
used up all of the hot water?

Take a vacation to a really cool place for Christmas but
have to spend two days at airports to get there and back

stay home and be bored in your pajamas
all day long on Christmas?

Would You Rather...

Find a dead bug floating in your
cup of hot chocolate

drink a cup of hot chocolate that someone dumped
a bottle of cinnamon into?

Open Christmas presents with your large family going
in order from oldest to youngest

find that your cat has already tore into
all your Christmas presents?

Would You Rather...

Drink a cup of hot chocolate after your dog
just slurped out of it

sit on a chair covered in freshly spilled hot chocolate?

Spend two whole days shopping for Christmas presents
with your mom but get everything you want for Christmas

spend two days playing in the snow instead and not get
a single present that you like?

Would You Rather...

Write a letter to Santa using a squeezy bottle of ketchup

by squeezing pickle juice from a big dill pickle?

Have Frosty the Snowman as your gym teacher so gym class is outside all winter long

play in gym class all winter long wearing your snow boots instead of sneakers?

Would You Rather...

Get missed by Santa Claus because
you are on vacation at Christmastime

get the same exact present from Santa
every single year of your life?

Eat a piece of fruitcake every meal
for an entire week

sleep on a block of hard fruitcake
instead of a pillow for a week?

Would You Rather...

Glue a bunch of cotton balls to your face
like Santa's beard

spend a day rolling around in a giant plastic ornament
like you're in a hamster ball?

Wear cheesy matching Christmas pajamas
with your family

grow a big fuzzy pair of reindeer antlers
out of your ears?

Would You Rather...

Be naughty and risk getting no presents from Santa

be the kid nobody likes because you're always telling them they'll end up on the naughty list?

Use $150 to buy the perfect presents
for your entire family

to buy something that you've really been wanting
for yourself?

Would You Rather...

Be Santa Claus and get the joy of delivering Christmas presents to children for Christmas

be Mrs. Claus and get the joy of keeping Santa Claus fat all year by feeding him cookies?

Live in a house made from yummy frosted gingerbread

inside of a house made out of creamy cold peppermint chocolate chip ice cream?

Would You Rather...

Grow a big large white fluffy beard
like Santa Claus

have a big jiggly jelly belly like Santa Claus?

Wake up and find coal in your stocking but cool toys
in your siblings' stockings

find pairs of socks and underwear in your stocking
on Christmas morning?

Would You Rather...

Wake up Christmas morning to find out that your stocking has disappeared and there are no presents from Santa for you

find a bunch of school supplies from Santa in your stocking?

Get the least number of presents in your whole family on Christmas morning

get a whole pile of really tiny little presents under the tree?

Would You Rather...

Have a nose that blinks red like Rudolph the Red Nosed Reindeer's every time you tell a lie

OR

have a really loud and annoying alarm go off every time you do something that puts you on the naughty list?

Spend a whole afternoon replacing burned out Christmas bulbs on ten strings of lights

OR

spend a whole evening driving around in the car with your family looking at lame Christmas light displays?

Would You Rather...

Believe that you are one of Santa's workshop elves and make everyone call you "Woody"

believe that you are a toy brought to life by Santa's magic and make everyone call you "Buddy"?

Get picked to sing a solo in your school's Christmas concert but have stage fright

sing the solo confidently until you embarrassingly blank out and forget the words to the song?

Would You Rather...

Have your hair turn snowy white
like Santa's

OR

find yourself saying "ho ho ho, Merry Christmas"
fifty times a day?

Have a family who takes "silent night" very seriously so
you can't talk at all on Christmas Eve

OR

have a family who spends all night on Christmas Eve
singing Christmas carols?

Would You Rather...

Grow big fluffy white Santa beards coming out of your armpits

one big white fluffy Santa beard coming out of your belly button?

Break a tooth eating a piece of your grandma's fruitcake

suffer a serious injury from the tape dispenser while wrapping Christmas presents?

Would You Rather...

Accidentally eat the last Christmas cookie before Christmas Eve so you have none to leave for Santa

accidentally eat half of the last cookie and leave the bitten off part sitting on a plate for Santa along with an apology note?

Sleep in a bed filled with crumbled sugar cookie crumbs

stick to your bed sheets because you are covered with gooey candy cane syrup?

Would You Rather...

Be forced by your parents to go to the shopping mall and take a picture with Santa Claus

be forced to dress up like a candy cane for the annual Christmas play?

SAY CHEESE!

Go Christmas shopping one hour a day for the whole month of December

read the same Christmas book before bed every night for the whole month of December?

Would You Rather...

Have a Christmas tree made
only of chewed bubble gum ornaments?

candy canes that have already been sucked on?

Listen to a bunch of out-of-tune Christmas carolers
for two hours

watch a two-hour long Christmas movie in a language
that you don't understand?

Would You Rather...

Have five strings of Christmas lights wrapped tightly around your whole body

crawl around on the floor underneath your Christmas tree picking up every single fallen needle?

Secretly unwrap and rewrap all of your presents before Christmas so you know what everything is

secretly trade name tags with one of your sibling's presents that you really want?

Would You Rather...

Sneeze every time you are around
a Christmas tree

break out with big red itchy bumps every time
you touch snow?

Spend twenty-four hours watching the same Christmas
show on repeat

sit in front of the TV for as long as it takes to watch every
Christmas show ever made?

Would You Rather...

Have the same annoying Christmas carol stuck in your head for a whole week

not be able to stop singing that same annoying Christmas carol nonstop for a whole day?

Spend an entire day walking around covered in Christmas lights from head to toe

go to sleep in a bedroom that has 2,000 Christmas lights strung from the ceiling and walls?

Would You Rather...

End every sentence with "fa-la-la"

begin every sentence with "ho-ho-ho"
in the month of December?

Wake up every morning to your little brother or sister
dipping your finger into a cup of warm hot chocolate

wake up every morning to your little brother or sister
dumping a bucket of cold snow onto your face?

Would You Rather...

Spend one hour straight licking
Christmas card envelopes

lick one envelope and get a huge papercut
on your tongue?

Dance in a fluffy tutu
for The Nutcracker ballet

go house to house in your neighborhood
singing Christmas carols?

Would You Rather...

Say "goody goody gumdrops" every time someone tells you a joke

OR

laugh with a hearty "ho ho ho"?

Build a gingerbread house using chewed bubble gum to "glue" it together

OR

eat a gingerbread house made from your dog's biscuits?

Would You Rather...

Open a bunch of Christmas presents covered with a ridiculous amount of sticky tape

presents that have been wrapped using rolls and rolls of toilet paper?

Live in the North Pole where there's no Wi-Fi or TV

be stranded on a tropical island with a cell phone that has 5% battery?

Would You Rather...

Have a Christmas with no presents
under the tree

an Easter with no candy in your Easter basket?

Get your most wished-for Christmas present and find out it
is broken and the stores are all closed so you can't return it

get a really ugly homemade Christmas sweater from your
aunt that you have to wear all day long?

Would You Rather...

Wear a sweater with jingle bells that tinkle
wherever you go

wear a pair of striped elf pants, pointy elf shoes,
and a tall floppy hat?

Eat a giant stack of sugar cookies drenched in maple syrup
for Christmas Day breakfast

a bunch of cardboard cookies covered with
super sweet frosting?

Would You Rather...

Spend twenty-four hours wrapped inside of a giant Christmas present

spend twenty-four hours carrying around a backpack filled with really heavy Christmas presents?

Celebrate Christmas with lots of presents except everyone is super crabby

celebrate a Christmas with only one present where everyone is super chilled and happy?

Would You Rather...

Have your mom post a really embarrassing picture
of you in your pjs on Christmas morning

accidentally break the special Christmas present you made
at school for your parents before you get to give it to them?

Have an all-out snowball fight with your friends using
only your left hand

ice skate for an hour balancing only on your left foot?

Would You Rather...

Accidentally break your mom's favorite Christmas ornament while decorating the tree

watch your little brother or sister step on your favorite ornament on purpose?

Eat a handful of bright yellow snow from your backyard

roll around in a pile of yellow snow wearing only your underpants?

Would You Rather...

Have red and white candy cane stripes
all over your body

a coating of gumdrop sugar that you can't wash off
of your body?

Have to share a bed with your little brother or sister
because you gave your room to Grandma and Grandpa
while they stay for Christmas

have to sleep on the couch with your dog snoring loudly
on the floor?

Would You Rather...

Never be able to get in the Christmas mood and say "bah humbug" all of the time

OR

walk around singing "Joy to the World" to everyone you meet?

Have your foot stomped on by one of Santa's Reight

OR

shovel a bunch of snow using only your hands and feet like a dog digging in the garden?

Would You Rather...

Spend a night outside in the snow with only your survival skills to build a fire and stay warm

accidentally get left home by yourself when your family leaves for Christmas vacation?

Wear socks that keep falling off inside of your snow boots

lose both of your mittens in a giant snowbank on a really cold day?

Would You Rather...

Have a red-light bulb on your head that lights up when you don't know the answer to a question

OR

have a green light bulb on your head that lights up when you do know the answer to a question?

Sit in a steamy warm outdoor hot tub on a really cold day

OR

take a long winter's nap in a cozy little snow cave?

Would You Rather...

Eat a dozen unfrosted
and tasteless sugar cookies

eat a dozen candy canes that have
no peppermint flavor at all?

Play a game of basketball wearing a pair of thick
and fuzzy mittens

play volleyball barefoot in the snow?

Would You Rather...

Have hard little reindeer hooves for feet that make it impossible to sneak up on anyone

OR

wear super big and pointy elf shoes on your feet that you keep tripping over?

Be snowed in at school overnight with your teacher and classmates

OR

get snowed out of a week of school but then have to go to school one week extra in the summer?

Would You Rather...

Eat a dozen sugar cookies frosted with mustard and ketchup

OR

suck on a pickle flavored candy cane?

Use a very poky pine branch to scratch a pesky itch on your back

OR

a candy cane as a spoon to try to eat your breakfast cereal?

Would You Rather...

Open all your presents like a crazy person in less than five minutes at Christmas

spend five very long and slow hours opening presents with your family?

Spend your recess helping sweaty little kids get their smelly snow gear on

playing freeze tag with your friends on a really cold day?

Would You Rather...

Begin every meal by eating a super minty candy cane

by drinking a giant glass of creamy eggnog?

Play on a playground that is covered with little round frozen rabbit poops

one that is covered with patches of yellow snow?

Would You Rather...

Be Santa Claus and get stuck inside of a chimney because you ate too many sugar cookies

turn black from head to toe because of all the coal in the chimneys you slid down?

Wear a red and black checkered flannel shirt that smells like a sweaty man

wear a hockey player's unwashed gear for the whole winter?

Would You Rather...

Wear a red and white furry Santa suit, complete with a big white beard, to the beach on a hot day

go outside during a blizzard wearing nothing but your swimsuit?

Soak your socks on the slushy playground and have to wear someone else's socks from the lost and found

soak your pants and have to wear someone else's pants from the lost and found?

Would You Rather...

Open a bunch of beautifully wrapped presents that have nothing in them

OR

get two awesome presents that look like they've been run over by Santa's sleigh?

Write a letter to Santa as a school project, rewriting it twenty times until your teacher says it's perfect

OR

write a quick letter to Santa misspelling the items on your list and getting the wrong things?

Would You Rather...

Drink a cup of hot chocolate while sitting
on a warm sunny beach

drink a cup of ice-cold lemonade while standing
in the middle of a big white snowbank?

Drink a gingerbread cookie
eggnog smoothie

eat a gingerbread cookie that is frosted with
eggnog icing?

Would you Rather...

Make a sled out of cardboard and spend an afternoon using it at the sledding hill

make a pair of ice skates using old shoes with butter knives attached and spend an afternoon at the skating rink?

Put a pinch of yellow snow in your hot chocolate to cool it off

drink a cup of hot chocolate with rock hard marshmallows floating all over it?

Would You Rather...

Play hide and seek by completely burying yourself
in snowbanks

play a game of high-speed tag on the ice-skating rink?

Fall off of your sled and tumble in a bunch of somersaults
all the way down the rest of the hill

climb all the way to the top of a big sledding hill
and accidentally drop your sled so it slides down
without you on it?

Would You Rather...

Play in sticky snow that sticks all over your whole body like glue

try to build a snowman with snow that melts the instant that you touch it?

Ride down a hill on the back of a sled where you can't see anything in front of you

ride on a sled tied to another sled so you can't control exactly where your sled is going?

Would You Rather...

Have the body of a
big misshapen lumpy snowman

the skinny twiggy arms of a snowman
that has no feet?

Know if you are on Santa's naughty list so you can
improve your behavior

always believe you are on Santa's good list even though
you sometimes aren't?

Would You Rather...

Spend your day ice fishing through a tiny hole in the ice not catching any fish

spend your day walking through the woods looking for a tree that you can cut down?

Spend three hours waiting in line with your little brother or sister to see Santa Claus at the shopping mall

wait in line to see Santa for two hours and then he has an emergency at the North Pole and has to leave for the day before you get to see him?

Would You Rather...

Have big fist-sized holes in the armpits of your winter jacket

lots of tiny holes in the thumbs of each of your mittens?

Dress up as an elf with your siblings and your parents as Mr. and Mrs. Claus for your annual family photo

have your faces put onto the bodies of Santa's reindeer for the annual family photo?

Would You Rather...

Be able to shoot snowballs
out of your belly button

have pine tree scented armpits?

Try to cut wrapping paper for your presents using your
fingers instead of scissors

wrap all your Christmas presents using chewed bubble
gum instead of scotch tape?

Would You Rather...

Wear a big fluffy hat made from
fake rabbit fur to school

a warm knitted hat that has two very large jingle bells
on top of it instead of a puff ball?

Eat a stale old gingerbread house leftover from
Christmas five years ago

eat a fruitcake from the year that you were born?

Would You Rather...

Wear winter scarves tied around your feet
instead of snow boots

wear snow boots on your hands instead of mittens?

Help out packing Christmas presents for
a Shoebox appeal before Christmas

help out collecting food to give to a foodbank
before Christmas?

Would you Rather...

Try to write out your homework using a pencil while wearing a pair of really puffy mittens

try to run a fast mile in gym class while wearing your overall snow pants?

Sit at a school desk which is covered in bright cheerful Christmas lights

use a chunk of coal instead of a pencil to do your homework?

Would You Rather...

Wear a winter jacket with a sticky zipper which is super hard to unzip

one size too big snow boots that are always falling off when you're walking through the snow?

Spend every day of your Christmas vacation shoveling snow from the sidewalks

spend every day of your Christmas vacation stuck in the house because you are snowed in?

Would You Rather...

Wear a backpack to school that has been stuffed
full of fluffy snow

wear a pair of boots that are filled with slushy snow?

Sleep underneath your Christmas tree to protect your
presents the whole month of December

have one of your presents disappear every day
for one week?

Would You Rather...

Live on a tropical island where it only snows
one day a year

in an Artic place where there is only one day a year
that it doesn't snow?

Take home a real Christmas tree that has a sleeping
squirrel inside of it

take home a Christmas tree that drops all its needles
on your floor overnight?

Would You Rather...

Have a sword fight using giant icicles
from your rooftop

splash in slushy snow puddles?

Have the friendly and magical Frosty the Snowman
for your teacher but not be able to use the classroom
heater or he'll melt

have Santa Claus who is so busy at the North Pole that
he usually has a substitute teacher in class for him?

Would You Rather...

Have to wear your big brother or sister's dirty and holey winter hand me downs

wear last year's snow pants that are so short they barely go below your knees?

Spend your afternoon pulling kids on their sleds up to the top of a snow hill

work as a skate monitor watching kids ice skate at the rink?

Would You Rather...

Turn completely white in the wintertime to camouflage your body with the white snow

turn completely green in the summertime to camouflage your body with the green grass?

Drink a hot cup of really watery hot chocolate

a too-chocolatey cup of way too cool hot chocolate?

Would You Rather...

Break your leg by slipping on a patch of slick ice and wear a cast all winter

get your tongue stuck to a metal fence pole and wear a bandage on it for two days?

Stick your tongue to a metal slide on the playground

have a bunch of snow stuffed down the back of your snow pants?

Would you Rather...

Faceplant into a big fluffy snowbank

step onto a frozen puddle and your foot breaks through into ice cold water?

POP!

Go outside during a snowstorm of paper snowflakes that give you a bunch of little, yet painful, papercuts

spend an hour pretending to play in a pile of fake snow for your family pictures?

Would You Rather...

Buy a package of candy canes and find that every single one is broken

buy a dozen gingerbread men and find that someone bit off every single head?

Spend five hours building a giant snow fort that completely melts in one day

build a super strong large snow fort that you and your family move into?

Would You Rather...

Hold the world record for making the most paper snowflakes in twenty-four hours

the world record for making the largest paper snowflake, one bigger than your house?

Spend all day trying to build a snow fort with snow that just crumbles apart

spend all day trying to build a sandcastle with dry sand that won't stick together?

Carve really amazing ice sculptures that always melt within a day

create amazing sand sculptures that get washed away by the tide every evening?

Play a game of baseball using snowballs instead of baseballs

play a game of dodgeball using snowballs instead of rubber balls?

Would You Rather...

Eat a bowl of Christmas tree
flavored ice cream

have a Christmas tree that smells like
peppermint candy canes instead of pine?

Get stuck in a blizzard where the electricity goes out and
you have no TV or video games

in a blizzard where your furnace goes out so there is no
heat and you have to wear all of your winter gear inside?

Would You Rather...

Skateboard on a really slippery ice-skating rink

play hockey while wearing a pair of roller skates?

Play soccer in the snow with a rock-hard frozen soccer ball

try to play volleyball using a beach ball on a really windy day?

Would You Rather...

Play a game of ice hockey using a frozen doughnut
instead of a puck

have a snowball fight using frozen cupcakes?

Wake up in the middle of the night to discover
Santa Claus delivering your presents

to discover your Elf on a Shelf moving
to a new hiding spot?

Would You Rather...

Sled down a giant snow hill
wearing a blindfold

try to play a game of ice hockey with the stick duct
taped to your hands?

Pull your friends around the playground on a big sled like
Santa's reindeer

work at the North Pole shoveling reindeer poo
for Santa Claus?

Would You Rather...

Eat a bowl of minty candy cane flavored oatmeal for breakfast

take a bath in a giant tube of creamy eggnogg?

Take care of Santa's reindeers by brushing them, feeding them, and pooper scooping their stalls

be the cook in charge of feeding all of Santa's elves at the workshop, some of whom are very picky eaters?

Would You Rather...

Shoot giant snowballs out of a snow cannon

icicles with an archery bow?

AIM*

* * * * * * * * * * * * * * * *

Have a giant blowup Christmas tree in your living room instead of a real tree

live with really grinchy parents who don't ever get in the Christmas spirit?

Would You Rather...

Find a bushy squirrel living in one of your snow boots

a tiny little mouse cuddled up in the thumb of your mitten?

Forget to water your Christmas tree so all its needles fall off before Christmas

overwater your Christmas tree until it gets a really funky smell to it?

Would You Rather...

Step on a broken Christmas ornament
and hurt your foot

trip into your Christmas tree and break
a whole bunch of ornaments but not hurt yourself?

Have to hand-draw every Christmas card that
you send to all your classmates

instead of sending Christmas cards donate money
to a charity?

Did You Enjoy
The Book ?

If you did, we are ecstatic. If not, please write your complaint to us and we will ensure we fix it.

If you're feeling generous, there is something important that you can help me with – tell other people that you enjoyed the book.

Ask a grown-up to write about it on Amazon. When they do, more people will find out about the book. It also lets Amazon know that we are making kids around the world laugh. Even a few words and ratings would go a long way.

If you have any ideas or jokes that you think are super funny, please let us know. We would love to hear from you.

Our email address is -
riddleland@riddlelandforkids.com

Riddleland Bonus

Join our **Facebook Group** at **Riddleland for Kids**
to get daily jokes and riddles.

https://pixelfy.me/riddlelandbonus

Thank you for buying this book. As a token of our appreciation,
we would like to offer a special bonus—a collection of
50 original jokes, riddles, and funny stories.

CONTEST

Would you like your jokes and riddles to be featured in our next book?

We are having a contest to discover the cleverest and funniest boys and girls in the world!

1) Creative and Challenging Riddles
2) Tickle Your Funny Bone Contest

Parents, please email us your child's "original" riddle or joke. He or she could win a Riddleland book and be featured in our next book.

Here are the rules:

1) We're looking for super challenging riddles and extra funny jokes.

2) Jokes and riddles MUST be 100% original—NOT something discovered on the Internet.

3) You can submit both a joke and a riddle because they are two separate contests.

4) Don't get help from your parents—UNLESS they're as funny as you are.

5) Winners will be announced via email or our Facebook group – **Riddleland for kids**

6) In your entry, please confirm which book you purchased.

Email us at **Riddleland@riddlelandforkids.com**

Other Fun Books by Riddleland
Riddles Series

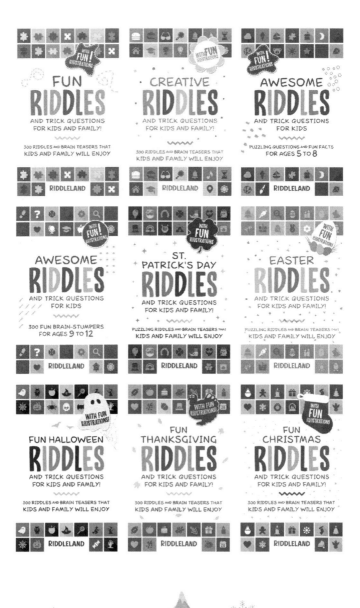

It's Laugh O'Clock Joke Books

Would You Rather...Series

Get them on Amazon or our website at
www.riddlelandforkids.com

ABOUT RIDDLELAND

Riddleland is a mum + dad run publishing company. We are passionate about creating fun and innovative books to help children develop their reading skills and fall in love with reading. If you have suggestions for us or want to work with us, shoot us an email at

riddleland@riddlelandforkids.com

Our favourite family quote

"Creativity is an area in which younger people have a tremendous advantage since they have an endearing habit of always questioning past wisdom and authority."

– Bill Hewlett

Made in the USA
Columbia, SC
13 December 2021

51353113R00063